HELPFUL HINTS FOR BORING MOMENTS

JUGGLING	4
WRITTEN CODES	8
SPOKEN CODES	10
SILENT SIGNALS	14
CONCORDE DARTS	18
CONCORDE HANGER	20
CEREAL PACKET SOCCER	22
BAT-A-RAT	26

BY JILL EGGLETON

ILLUSTRATED BY MATTHEW THOMPSON

Helpful Hints for Boring Moments

SCENARIO:

It is Saturday. The rain is pouring from leaden clouds.

You watch it, running like a river down the windowpane, overflowing the drains and making puddles in your backyard. You can't go outside. There is nothing that interests you on television. You have read all your books, and seen all the videos in your video collection.

You are bored!

bored!

bored!

DO YOU:

- eat a bowl of ice cream and a packet of marshmallows?

- paint on the window with toothpaste?

- construct a flying machine from the dining-room table?

NO!

But you could make some juggling balls and learn to juggle . . .

QUESTION:

What do you think could be sensible activities to do when you are stuck inside?

JUGGLING

yeee haaa!

HOW TO MAKE JUGGLING BALLS:

PROCEDURE:

You will need:
3 old socks
dried beans
a needle and thread

STEPS:

- Cut the toe ends off the socks.

- Fill the toe ends about three-quarters full with the dried beans.

- Sew up the open ends.

HOW TO JUGGLE WITH 3 BALLS:

A Start with ball 1 and ball 3 in your left hand, and ball 2 in your right hand.

B Throw ball 1 up in an arc towards your right hand.

C Throw ball 2 towards your left hand before ball 1 arrives in your right hand.

D As soon as you have caught ball 1, throw ball 3 towards your right hand, over the arc made by ball 2.

E Catch ball 2 in your left hand.

F Catch ball 3 in your right hand.

G Start again from the right-hand side.

QUESTION:

What do you think makes these instructions difficult to follow?

What helps make them easier?

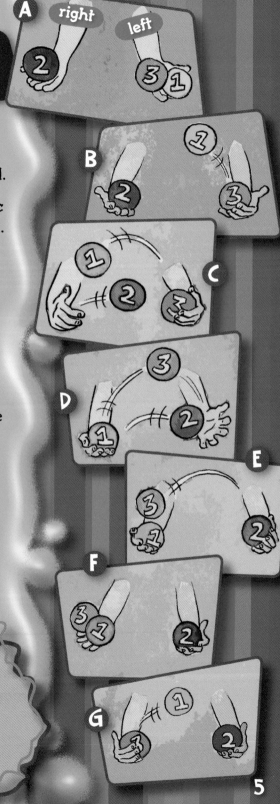

5

SCENARIO:

You have the measles. Hundreds of red spots cover your entire body. You resemble an alien from a distant planet.

You have been given medicine that tastes like licorice and peppermint, and smells like cowpats. The doctor said you must stay home, and in bed. You lie there, thinking of all the things you will miss – the book your teacher is reading, the play you are in, and the rendezvous you'd planned with your friend after school.

You are bored!

bored!

bored!

DO YOU:

- pull all the feathers out of your pillow?

- tie your sheets into knots?

- use your mum's cellphone to ring all your friends?

NO!

But you could practise written code messages and send them to a friend . . .

CLARIFY: RENDEZVOUS

A secret plan

B appointment

C expedition

A, B OR C?

WRITTEN CODES

Simple Cipher:
A cipher is the coding of a message using letters to stand for other letters.

HOW TO WRITE WRITTEN CODES:

PROCEDURE:

1. Write the letters of the alphabet out on one line.

2. Write the alphabet again, directly below the first alphabet line, but start with **D**, and end with **C**.

3. Use the letters from the top line for the word you want to code, and the bottom line to create your code.

    e.g. F I S H
         I L V K

A	B	C	D	E	F	G	H	I	J	K	L	M	N	O	P	Q	R	S	T	U	V	W	X	Y	Z

D	E	F	G	H	I	J	K	L	M	N	O	P	Q	R	S	T	U	V	W	X	Y	Z	A	B	C

You could send this message:

VWOB OZOB
L KOYH WKH PHOVOHV

(You will have to keep the code a secret, because nosey brothers or sisters will soon decipher it!)

OR

You could practise spoken code messages and teach a friend later . . .

sshh!

CLARIFY: DECIPHER

A discover

B decode / uncode

C copy

A, B OR C?

9

SPOKEN CODES

HOW TO SPEAK IN PIG LATIN:

RULES:

- For words beginning with a vowel, add **WAY** at the end.

- For words beginning with a consonant, blend or digraph, take the sound to the end of the word, and add **AY**.

How quickly can you work out what this says?

ALKINGTAY IKELAY ISTHAY ANCAY
IVEDRAY EOPLEPAY ANANASBAY

HOW TO MAKE UP YOUR OWN CODE:

You can make up your own secret language to use with your friends. The odder it sounds, the better.

Why not try **OSH** before vowels? You would drive people bananas with words like bananas.

BOSHANOSHANOSHAS!!

anannasbay

ikelay

alkingtay

QUESTION:

When do you think people would find it useful to talk in code?

SCENARIO:

You and your sister are in a café with your mum and her friends.

They are discussing cooking, the weather, and beauty treatments. Your mum's friend has just had a facial. You have no idea what a facial is, but it sounds horrific. It definitely doesn't sound like something you would want. You've finished your hot chocolate and you're bored.

You are bored!

bored!

bored! bored!

... facial

... the weather

blah blah...

SYNONYM:

A word or term that has the same meaning as another word or term.

Can you find a synonym for the word 'horrific'?

DO YOU:

- make planes from the serviettes and fire them around the café?

- turn the salt and pepper shakers upside down?

- play feet games with your sister under the table?

NO!

But you could send your sister silent signals . . .

SILENT SIGNALS

HOW TO SEND MORSE CODE BLINK SIGNALS:

You will have to memorise the Morse code alphabet.

A ●—	H ●●●●	O ———	V ●●●—
B —●●●	I ●●	P ●——●	W ●——
C —●—●	J ●———	Q ——●—	X —●●—
D —●●	K —●—	R ●—●	Y —●——
E ●	L ●—●●	S ●●●	Z ——●●
F ●●—●	M ——	T —	? ●●——●●
G ——●	N —●	U ●●—	

Now send a message!

Blink for a count of one = dot

Blink for a count of three = dash

Stare = END OF MESSAGE

14

HOW TO SEND A HAND SIGNAL MESSAGE:

You will have to learn these hand signals.

 A

 B

 C

 D

 E

 F

 G

 H

 I

 J

 K

 L

 M

 N

 O

 P

 Q

 R

 S

 T

 U

 V

 W

 X

 Y

Z

QUESTION:

When do you think hand signal messages could be used?

15

SCENARIO:

Your cousins have come to stay for the night – all five of them!

Your mother said you have to entertain them because they are in your house. They are rowdy and rambunctious! You can't go outside, it's too dark. They follow you into your room and fiddle with your gear. You put on a computer game, but they can't agree who should play. You get out board games, but they don't like board games. You turn on the television, but they don't like television. In fact, they hate sitting still.

They are bored and you are bored!

bored!

bored!

DO YOU:

- imagine the beds are trampolines and jump up and down?

- turn off all the lights and chase each other through the house?

- play soccer with your mother's cushions?

NO!

But you could make super-fast concorde darts . . .

CLARIFY:
RAMBUNCTIOUS

- **A** wild / lively
- **B** rude
- **C** bad-mannered

A, B OR C?

CONCORDE DARTS

HOW TO MAKE A CONCORDE DART:

MATERIALS:

1 sheet of paper (A4)

DIRECTIONS:

1. Fold the sheet of paper in half lengthways to make a crease. Then unfold it.

2. Fold in corners **A** and **B** to the crease.

3. Fold in corners **C** and **D** to the crease.

4. Fold the dart in half along the crease.

5. Fold down one side to the central fold.

6. Turn the dart over and do the same again.

HOW TO FLY THE DART:

Hold the dart underneath with your thumb and forefinger.
Aim and throw!

OR

You could make a concorde hanger . . .

QUESTION:

What other materials do you think you could use to make a dart? Why?

What materials would you not use to make a dart? Why not?

throw it!

19

CONCORDE HANGER

HOW TO MAKE A CONCORDE HANGER:

EQUIPMENT:

- 4 wire coat hangers
- sticky tape
- string
- open door

PROCEDURE:

1. Bend the coat hangers into diamond shapes.

2. Tie one end of the piece of string onto the hook of a coat hanger.

3. Tape the other end of the string to the door frame.

go!

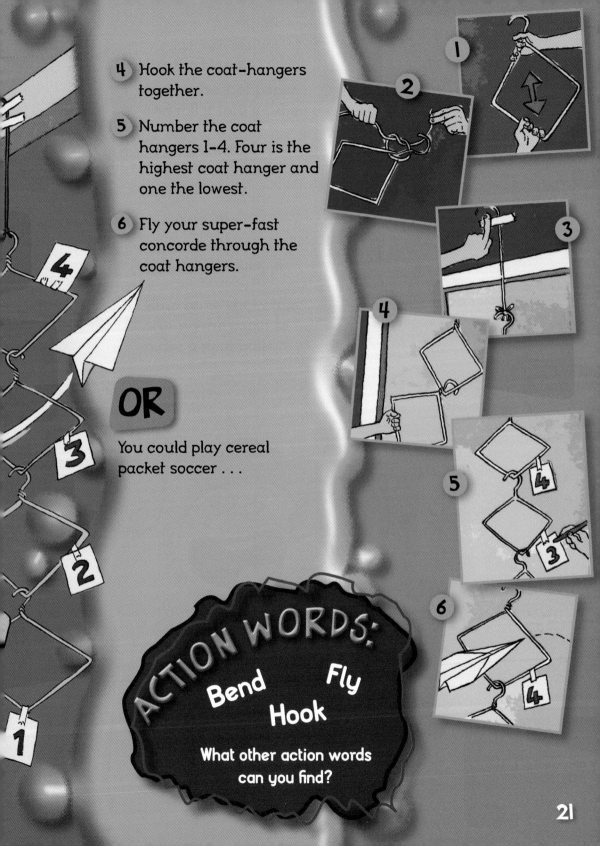

4. Hook the coat-hangers together.

5. Number the coat hangers 1–4. Four is the highest coat hanger and one the lowest.

6. Fly your super-fast concorde through the coat hangers.

OR

You could play cereal packet soccer . . .

ACTION WORDS:

Bend   Fly

Hook

What other action words can you find?

CEREAL PACKET SOCCER

HOW TO MAKE A CEREAL PACKET SOCCER GAME:

MATERIALS:

- empty cereal packet
- sticky tape
- glue
- scissors
- sheets of paper

cool!

PROCEDURE:

Making the Goals

1 Cut the cereal packet in half.

2 Cut the front and back out of each half to make a goal area.

3 Place a sheet of paper on the floor, and tape the goals at each end.

Making the blower

1 Take a sheet of paper and roll it into a tube.

2 Tape the tube.

Making the ball

1 Scrunch some paper up into a small ball.

2 Wrap some sticky tape around the paper to make a neat ball.

PREDICT:

How do you think this game will be played?

23

HOW TO PLAY CEREAL PACKET SOCCER:

- Divide into two teams.

- Each team selects a goal.

- Using your blower, try and blow the ball into the other team's goal.

- The first team to get 21 goals is the winner.

RULES:

- If a player blows the ball off the pitch, the other team blows it in.

- No touching the ball with your hands.

- No using a vacuum cleaner or bike pump to blow the ball.

ONLY THE BLOWER!

OR

You could make a bat-a-rat game . . .

let's play!

QUESTION:

Why do you think it is necessary to include rules in instructions of how to play something?

?

BAT-A-RAT

HOW TO MAKE A BAT-A-RAT GAME:

EQUIPMENT:

- 2 newspapers
- sticky tape
- a chair
- small, soft, unbreakable objects for the rats

PROCEDURE:

Roll up one of the newspapers quite loosely and tape it with sticky tape to make a tube. Tape the tube to the back of a chair.

Fold the other newspaper in half, roll it up and tape it to make the bat.

wooo hoo!

HOW TO PLAY BAT-A-RAT:

One player drops the rats down the tube on the chair (one at a time). The other player tries to hit them with the bat as they fall out the bottom.

RULES:

Each player has ten hits. A point is scored only if the rat is hit.

QUESTION:

How else do you think you could play the bat-a-rat game?

THINK ABOUT THE TEXT

What connections can
you make to the text?

overcoming
frustration

thinking
logically

interpreting
instructions

TEXT TO
SELF

relieving
boredom

having fun

following
procedure

TEXT TO TEXT

Think about other texts you may have read that have similar features. Compare the texts.

TEXT TO WORLD

Talk about situations in the world that might connect to elements in the story.

PLANNING A PROCEDURAL TEXT

THINK ABOUT . . .

Who will be reading the text.

THINK ABOUT . . .

The purpose of the text. Is it to:

show how to make something?

show how to do something?

show how to play something?

show how to use something?

THINK ABOUT . . .

What information the reader will need to carry out the procedure.

A sequence that will make sense – which should come first, next . . . ?

How to make	Statement of Goal	Materials	Steps in Order →
How to do	Statement of Goal		Steps in Order →
How to use	Statement of Goal		Steps in Order →
How to play	Statement of Goal		Steps in Order →

THINK ABOUT . . .

How you can make your procedural text clear and easy to follow.

Use photographs, diagrams, maps, cross-sections . . .

Use numbered steps, bullet points . . .

Use lists

Use headings and subheadings to organise the information

PROCEDURAL TEXTS USUALLY HAVE

- opening goals or aims, for example,

  How to . . .

  Making a . . .

- action verbs, for example, cut, start, fill, throw, write, make . . .

- clear, concise language that is easy to follow

- words that indicate sequence – next, after, then, before . . .

- present or future tense

- lists of materials or ingredients needed

- headings, diagrams, drawings, photographs, maps, labels, tables, illustrations, bullets, arrows, captions, numbers . . .

- rules or guidelines